blessings
BELINDA BROWN

Copyright © 2013 HGPUK Belinda Brown

Heathrow Gateway Publishing UK All rights reserved. No part of this book may be reproduced, stored in a retrieval system, or transmitted in any form or by any means, electronic, mechanical, photocopying, recording, scanning, or otherwise, without the prior written permission of the publisher.

Disclaimer

All the material contained in this book is provided for educational and informational purposes only. No responsibility can be taken for any results or outcomes resulting from the use of this material. While every attempt has been made to provide information that is both accurate and effective, the author does not assume any responsibility for the accuracy or use/misuse of this information.

**Publishing rights administered on Amazon by HGPUK
All rights reserved**

Published in the United Kingdom by
Heathrow Gateway Publishing UK
Heathrow House, London
United Kingdom
Tel: UK: +447424668890
Tel: US: +12027549093
Email: hgpuk@gmail.com
Web: www.joshuajogo.com

*T*HIS BOOK is dedicated to my husband Ian who has always encouraged and advised me; to my daughter Carmen, who has grown to be my best friend and to my son Euan who has always been my biggest supporter.

This is to acknowledge the internationally renowned British Master Perfumer Roja Dove, the world's most quoted fragrance expert and founder of the illustrious Roja Dove Haute Parfumerie at Harrods. Also to Matthew Marriott for his extraordinary patience and design skills.

Without their help and guidance 'Blessings' would simply not exist.

There is a well known story in the Bible about Jesus healing ten lepers and yet only one of them came back to thank Him. So, learning from that, I would like to thank everyone who stuck by me in good times and bad and helped me on my way. Thank you and I hope you'll enjoy this book as much as I enjoyed putting it together.

. . . . .

blessings
BELINDA BROWN

*S*ome things are heaven scent
the remarkable story of Belinda Brown

by Belinda Brown
in conversation with Paul Cooper

WHEN I STARTED to recollect the days of my childhood and my life in West Africa where I was born and raised, I must confess to shedding tears at some of the events that have shaped my life and that led me to where I am today. For someone like me, brought up with a strong Christian faith, my story can be explained by way of a divine plan, my God shaping and guiding my every step. For others, it may just seem a series of remarkable coincidences that, in turn, saved my life, introduced me to the those who would be my inspiration and led me to becoming Africa's first black female luxury perfumer. Whatever your beliefs, I hope you find my story interesting and that, in some small way it may inspire you to follow your dreams.

From my earliest recollections, the Bible story of Mary anointing Jesus's feet with fragrant Alabaster oils has remained with me and the scents and fragrances of my childhood have lodged themselves in my subconscious. It was the quest to unlock those memories that stirred such strong emotions in me and led to the creation of 'Blessings'.

The name for my perfume range was obvious from the start because, despite the trials and disasters that have come my way, I am blessed to be where I am today.

Belinda Brown.

• • • • •

blessings

contents

Genesis   ONE
in the beginning

Exodus   SEVENTEEN
we leave Africa for England

Chronicles   TWENTY NINE
I start to form a plan

Acts   THIRTY NINE
"Blessings" becomes a reality

Revelations   FORTY NINE
my inspirational journey

. . . . .

Genesis
in the beginning

I WAS BORN Belinda Osoru in 1965 in Ghana, in West Africa.

We were not rich, but neither were we poor, due in the most part to my wonderful Mother Janet, who worked tirelessly to provide for me and my siblings. My father Jimmy was a sailor, so spent a lot of time away from home.

My Mother was unable to read and write because, although her Father was himself an educated man, custom dictated that, as the eldest daughter, she could not attend school and had to stay at home to look after the house. She was determined that I would not suffer the same fate so, when I was five years old, a major family upheaval took place. Whilst my Father stayed at the village where his work was, the rest of us moved to Nigeria.

My eldest brother Bon, went to live with an uncle in Lagos and my Mother took me and my smaller brother and sister with her to stay with some other relatives in the city, until we found our feet.

Now you must understand that I mean "relatives" in the broadest sense of the word. West Africa was and still is, a tight community where everyone tends to know everyone else and "uncles" and "aunts" are everywhere.

The city was a dangerous place and we were warned not to talk to strangers and especially not to accept food from someone we did not know. One day however - a day I shall never forget - I saw one of our "aunts" offering a handful of food to my younger brother and sister. I ran screaming to my Mother who rushed to her children and tried desperately to remove the food from their mouths. I shall never know for certain whether the food was poisoned but, that night my younger sister Amanda contracted a fever and after several hours, she died.

My younger brother Dorban, died two days later.

For some reason I was spared.

• • • • •

TWO

"Africa...
Where it all began

2

blessings

MY MOTHER AND I fled across the Niger Delta to the large town of Warri. The journey took all day by boat (it takes 20 minutes for the same journey by road today) and on reflexion we did not speak the local language, cannot have had any money nor any real idea where we were going.

My Father joined us when he could, which tended to liven things up as he was an extremely generous man and kept bringing back waifs and strays to stay at our house. He would feel sorry for them and invite them back for a good meal and a rest. Wonderful gestures, but hard on my Mother and me.

We picked up the local dialect and soon I was ready for school. The main criterion for entry was that you could touch your right ear by putting your left arm over your head. I passed!

Because of the time it had taken for us to settle in and find our feet, I was a year behind the others, but soon made up the time as I found lessons fun. Mother became pregnant and in 1974, my little brother Dorban (named after my beloved other little brother who had died) was born.

• • • • •

Obviously with my Mother working all hours to provide for us, I became a de facto "mum" at the age of 10, caring for Dorban after school until my Mother came home. Out of necessity therefore, my Mother became a strong willed and resourceful woman and set about making a home for us and providing as best she could. She would work all hours buying this and selling that, making clothes and bags and selling them in the marketplace. I would go with her and help so, from a very early age, the sights and smells of life in Warri were all around me. Spices, herbs, ripe mangos - everything combined in a heady, unforgettable mixture.

Other not so pleasant smells also invaded my world. Growing up in this oil producing area, my friends and I would have to hold our noses as Warri was hit by fumes from gas flaring operations that created huge volumes of nauseous 'greenhouse' emissions. At home, though, I could take refuge in a very special and comforting aroma: that of a favourite moisturising cream named Stella Pomade, a rich mixture of lavender, jasmine and vanilla. My Mother would massage me from head to toe with Stella, which has been a skin care choice of many Nigerians for more than three decades. She would also shower when she came home and then cover herself with a white powder that I remember also had a wonderful aroma.
It made me feel so happy and lucky because, in my world, very few people could afford perfume of any kind.

A seed had been sown.

• • • • •

"My parents & me in Warri

3

I SAT AND PASSED the Common Entrance Exam and was awarded a place at Horsey College but this was a fee-paying school. For the first term all was well but then money got really tight and my Mother could no longer keep up the pretence that we could afford such an education. I left.

I then had to re-sit the Common Entrance Exam which I again passed and applied to go to a training college which was paid for by the State as long as students became teachers at the end of the course. With all the delay in re-sitting exams, I was once again a year behind the others. I worked at night to help with the family funds and stayed at the college until I passed my final exams at the age of 18 despite contracting typhoid in my final year.

I was then sent to Bomadi School as a student teacher. As this was a day's boat ride away from home I tended to stay there during the holidays with a couple of friends rather than make the arduous journey back to my Mother.

By this time however, I was getting to be as determined and resourceful as her.

• • • •

blessings

I started to do all sorts of things to make money. I sold lottery tickets, I bought and sold rice, tomatoes and oil and, when I went to Church choir practice, there was always something in my bag to sell or exchange.

Then one day I collapsed with the most extraordinary pain in my side. Friends asked what was wrong, but all I knew was that I needed help. When the pain got too much they rushed me to hospital where I was diagnosed with a perforated appendix and I knew I was in a life threatening situation but I had no money for expensive medical treatment.

Amazingly, a friend of my eldest brother, whom I had not seen for years, recognised me. He had an insurance medical card so he suggested I pretend that I was his wife so that my treatment would be covered under his insurance. This I did and duly underwent an emergency operation which I believe saved my life. The drama was not over as I was then discharged with nowhere to go to convalesce. I tried to contact relatives but no one would help.

As I sat slumped and in tears outside the hospital my friend Mary just happened to pass by in her car. She took me in, let me stay with her until I was fully fit.

Again, something or "someone" had intervened.

• • • •

TEN

Everything in the market combined in a heady, unforgettable mixture

4

I KNEW IN MY HEART that teaching was not for me - that I wanted something different for myself. So I went back to college and sat and passed my 'A' level exams in accountancy and business studies.

News came through that my Father had died back home in his village. A good man who had always tried his best to help and please others.

By now I had a strong self-belief. I knew I needed to escape from teaching in a small school in the Delta. There was a whole world out there and the gateway to this world was - the International Airport!

So, I applied to be a stewardess and was rejected. I applied for a position in customs - again to no avail. Finally - and to this day I really do not know how it happened - I was accepted for a post in security which, at the time, had shades of 'James Bond' about it and I was very excited to be part of this undercover world!

The airport seemed so exotic with the constant coming and going of international travellers with their fashionable clothes and accessories. Of course I was drawn to the Duty Free area - to the smell of high end fragrances and perfumes and vowed that, one day I would shop there and indulge myself. But how?

Then one day I was approached by an obviously successful and important looking white business man who informed me that he had picked up the wrong case by mistake from the carousel. He instructed me (no other description will do) that, if and when the mistake was discovered and the other passenger returned to the airport to exchange bags, that I should immediately take a taxi to his office and deliver the correct bag personally to him. He said his firm (a major oil company) would reimburse any expenses. He left me his card.

I didn't know what to do but soon the situation escalated as a breathless black man came running up the concourse clutching a case and looking very distressed. He was delighted when I returned his rightful case to him.
I now had a problem.

I just could not bring myself to return the case alone, so I persuaded a colleague to come with me for support. We duly took a taxi and made our way to the address on the business card. The offices were very plush and our businessman obviously very important. True to his word he thanked us profusely and more than covered the cost of the taxi; in fact he gave us a generous tip for our trouble.

. . . . .

FOURTEEN

"Signing the register

Time went by and I thought no more about it until one evening I was nagged and nagged by a friend to go to a party. Now I didn't usually go out in the evening due to the rather secretive side to my job and the risks that it entailed but, for some reason I decided to go. Among the guests was a face I felt looked familiar but that I couldn't place for the life of me. I went over to a friend who was standing almost next to the man I had recognised and asked in our local dialect who he was. Thinking we were speaking in a language no one else could understand I tried to explain that I was sure I knew him from somewhere. Imagine my surprise when he interrupted us and, speaking fluently in our dialect, refreshed my memory. He was the businessman whose case I had returned earlier that year.

After that meeting we dated secretly for six months until we could stand the hiding away no longer.

So, I resigned from my job with airport security, became Mrs Ian Brown and moved to Lagos.

• • • • •

SIXTEEN

5

*L*IFE BECAME HECTIC. I worked in a variety of jobs and kept my promise to myself by spending my spare money on perfume.

When I accompanied Ian on one of his business trips I would purchase a couple of perfumes I had never tried before and, like my Mother before me, would shower when I got home and cover myself in delicious fragrances before I went to bed. A habit that would last a lifetime.

When we went on holiday, I always made sure that I tried to seek out the local fragrances and some have become important to me.

In India for example, I bought a highly concentrated 'attar' - an Arabic word which means 'scent'. I was told that the story of Indian perfumes is as old as the civilization itself. From earliest times, scented oils were extracted by pressing, crushing or distilling aromatic flowers and vegetables. Archeological surveys have revealed round copper stills, used for the distillation process, that are at least 5000 years old These stills are called degs. Following the flowering season, traditional attar makers, with their degs, travelled all over India to make their perfumes.

Even now, a few traditional attar makers still travel to be close to the harvest. Their equipment has changed little, if at all over the years. Also the truly fabulous bergamot I encountered in India gave me the idea for the colours for my first perfume as the beautiful foliage and pale pink flowers are surrounded by the most amazing purple leaves.

In Oman I first encountered the wonderful frankincense trees. Now frankincense was one of the consecrated incenses mentioned in the Song of Solomon in the Bible and was, of course, one of the gifts the wise men from the East brought the infant Jesus. The frankincense produced in Oman is probably the finest in the World. Needless to say I had to be restrained from buying far too much!

In Granada, the spice island in the Caribbean, I visited the market and found the colours and fragrances to be overwhelming. I sat for hours with a dear old lady and talked and talked about my love and passion for perfumes. Another priceless addition to my education.

Finally on a trip to Grasse, the perfume capital of France, I came across jasmine for the first time and simply fell in love with it. It is so expensive because thousands of flowers are needed to produce each gramme of oil. Jasmine, along with rose oil, would become the most important and costly ingredients of my future perfume range.

• • • • •

blessings

TWENTY

Exodus
we leave Africa for England

1

*I*N 2001 Ian and I, together with our two children Carmen and Euan, left Nigeria for Sussex, England. The children were educated in the excellent local schools, we had a lovely house and a garden that always inspired me and I made friends quickly at the children's school and church. Life was good and yet I still wanted to pursue something by myself. I ran a property business in Nigeria always supported by Ian who offered me sound advice and guidance. When it became too difficult to run the business from afar, I thought about fashion. Maybe clothes with an African twist or designer shoes and slippers? But one thought had been with me since childhood - perfume.

When I first chatted to my friends about making my own perfume, they were very wary and tried to point out all the difficulties I would face. Surely they said, that was only for celebrities, experts, or companies with endless funds to invest and anyway, where on earth would I start?

· · · · ·

2

My daughter Carmen was growing up to be just like me and when she bought her first bottle of perfume on a school trip to France, I was cross with her until my son Euan reminded me of the array of perfumes on my dressing table and that she was simply following my lead. He was right, I was wrong and Carmen got an apology. I took this as another sign that here was where my future lay.

We continued to travel a lot and each new place we visited added to my knowledge and interest in the subject.

For example, when I was in New York with Carmen and we wandered down glorious Fifth Avenue, we saw this one particular bottle being displayed in a window. We entered the beautiful shop to find out more about this bottle. Once holding it and feeling the quality of the glass I enquired as to the price. No doubt a bottle as striking as this, with such great quality would cost an absolute fortune. It did!

When we visited the Bordeaux region of France we came across a small shop similar to a pharmacy, where you could mix oils to create your own fragrance. Carmen and I were in heaven!

On a later holiday in Kenya, I met up with a lady that had grown close to my family. She is Italian by blood, but Kenyan at heart and she was a great source of information about Kenyan perfume and scented oils, so I began to quiz her to find out all she knew. She revealed to me a local oil manufacturer and suggested I pay them a visit.

I had to take an incredibly long trip to the North of Kenya which, when I finally arrived, amazed me because, as the plant life was so different, they were able to create completely unique scents and oils from those I was used to.

I was attracted by how pure all the ingredients were and I was amazed at all the natural African substances that could be used. I had tended to use Frankincense and Myrrh throughout my time in Kenya with my family, but once returning back home to England, I stopped using them for a while. One evening however, I wore them again at dinner and my son ran into the room saying "Mummy, I can smell Africa!"

My childhood memories had just received an endorsement from the next generation!

. . . . .

TWENTY FOUR

3

WHEN THE exciting trips to fabulous places dried up for a while, I must admit to feeling a bit lost and it took me some time to get my focus back. But once I did, there was no stopping me.

I began experimenting with essential oils bought on-line, but soon realised that this was a very tricky business and it was not until an aromatherapist friend showed me that it could be done that I knew that, if I could find the expertise from somewhere, I could create something special and unique to me. But where do you find that expertise? How do you start to attempt to break into a market that no black African woman had ever entered before? Clearly it needed another miracle.

4

*I*N 2006 came news that devastated me. My older brother Bon had died. He had always been my rock, someone I could always turn to wherever he was.

Because of our childhood memories of being separated, we had remained very close and always told each other everything. His life had been difficult as he suffered an early setback which knocked him off course for a while. He had been very bright and had earned a scholarship to Alabama State University in the USA. Everything was planned and everyone very excited for him when, at the very last minute and with no explanation whatsoever, his place at the University was withdrawn. He had no choice but to find work locally and spent some time at the Port Authority which he really did not like.

Eventually with a lot of hard work and dedication he rose to become one of the top crop scientists of his generation and we were all very proud of him.

I missed him then and I still miss him today but his death made me even more determined to be successful and to make him proud of me.

. . . . .

"the beginning of my dream...
the Roja Dove Haute Parfumerie
HARRODS

Chronicles
I start to form a plan

1

*M*Y FRIEND SHADIDA had worked at Harrods and so I went to see her and we chatted about my ideas and dreams and she agreed to give it some thought.

My only lead was to recall that, in Lagos some years ago, I had met an amazing Egyptian woman. The first time I came in contact with her I was struck by the fact that she smelt incredible. I asked her if I could pay her a visit to learn more about the scent she was wearing. Two days later I found myself in her house somewhere in Ikoyi about 10 minutes away from my house at the time.

She really opened my eyes to the wonders of perfume and she became a good friend. So.. why not go to Egypt and visit her to see if I could take inspiration from her as I had once before?

I contacted her, the visit was arranged and the flights booked, when Shadida phoned out of the blue very, very excited. She had popped into the food hall at Harrods and, quite by chance had bumped into Roja Dove of all people!

I went very quiet as the name meant absolutely nothing to me. Shadida calmed down and patiently explained that Roja was the foremost perfume expert in the country, that he was an Internationally renowned "nose", that he ran the exclusive Roja Dove Haute Parfumerie within the Urban Retreat at Harrods and that she had told him all about my passion. He was expecting my call to arrange a meeting!

This I duly did by making the date through his office, but then had to go back to Nigeria to sort out my property business which was really suffering with me being so far away and funds were mysteriously disappearing leaving me in a very difficult position financially. Because of all these problems, I decided to wind the business up, but all this took time and I realised to my horror that I was not going to make my meeting with Roja. In a state of panic and trepidation I telephoned him from Nigeria and he could not have been nicer, telling me not to worry and that he would see me any time I was back and could get up to London. What a relief!

• • • • •

Roja

2

*S*HADIDA WENT WITH ME for my first meeting with Roja and, after the introduction left the two of us to talk.. and talk and talk!

During that first four hour meeting we discussed everything from the meaning of life, through my Christian faith and the story of Mary and Alabaster oils, to my childhood and passion for fragrances.

He talked me through the processes for making a new perfume and kindly and patiently let me try and sample some of the wonderful fragrances he had produced. He then asked me to point out the fragrance that was most like those I had remembered from my childhood. My answer was simple - it was not in that room! At this point Roja seemed genuinely excited and we discussed the essence of the smells that had surrounded me form childhood and, of course, the Stella Pomade that my mother had introduced to me all those years ago. I decided to return to Nigeria, bring back the Stella Pomade and try to replicate those evocative African fragrances that meant so much to me.

I was on a mission!

. . . . .

3

WHEN I GOT BACK HOME I explained to my husband all the plans that were whirring around in my head. He was really supportive but, at the same time urged caution as he well knew the difficult road that lay ahead. He understood however that, whether by luck or divine intervention, the assistance and expertise of Roja Dove was a priceless asset.

Roja himself could not have been more supportive and was always on hand to patiently help me achieve my goal which, at that time, was still simply to produce a perfume for Belinda Brown. He arranged for me to spend a day smelling all the oils and finding one that I loved. I found this really really hard.

Each time I tried a fragrance, I would tell Roja my instant opinion - whether I liked or hated it, what it said to me and how I would describe it. He would write this all down and from these notes he would amazingly be able to tell my mood that day - if I was happy or sad, energetic or tired. He would then take my favourite fragrances back to his laboratory and blend them into a range of say five or six perfumes for me to sample.

This went on for months until, bit by bit, we narrowed the choices down.

"Roja's advice and expertise have been priceless"

4

MY EDUCATION in perfume making included how to master the relative volatility of each perfume oil.

I also grasped the "notes" that you need to combine to produce the desired effect. Top notes consist of a small molecule that evaporates quickly. Middle notes are the main body of the perfume which becomes more pleasant with time (they can also be called the heart notes) and finally the base notes bring out the depth and solidity to a perfume. They reflect the class of the scent and are typically rich and deep, not usually perceived until 30 minutes after application.

blessings

5

AFTER A WHILE, when things were progressing and we were close to perfecting my "fragrance of African memories" Roja asked why I was keeping it for myself - had I considered marketing it - maybe at first for my friends but then, perhaps to a wider audience. I was amazed. Where would I sell it and who would stock it?

Surely not the World's most famous department store in Knightsbridge, London?

THIRTY SIX

blessings

My Alabaster Jar

Acts

"Blessings" becomes a reality

1

IF I WAS TO seriously bring "Blessings" to the marketplace, I would need help in marketing, packaging and bottle design - all those important areas that would create the essence of my "brand". But where to start?

The school my children attended had just produced a really beautifully designed brochure and it had impressed everyone, including me. I had no idea who had done the design and production work but one evening, at a school function, my daughter pointed out a man to me who she said was her Sunday School teacher and that she was sure he had told her that he had designed the school brochure. She seemed absolutely certain so I took the opportunity of approaching him.

My working relationship with Matthew Marriott was born.

• • • • •

2

MATTHEW STARTED WORK on creating the image for "Blessings" and it was clear from the beginning that we were both perfectionists. We strived to find that perfect balance between a modern design for our packaging and yet to also convey quality. My journey with Roja was also moving towards fruition as at last I was happy that I had captured the fragrance of my memory. Combining jasmine with rose de mai picked on the hillsides of southern France, together with notes of bergamot, lemon and mandarin, and tonka bean, vanilla and warm cedar, I was confident we had succeeded - Blessings 'Purple' had arrived.

Roja's team led by the wonderful Jamie, also helped me source bottles from bespoke glass manufacturers in the Czech Republic. Alabaster is a rock that has been used to carve into jars to hold perfume for thousands of years and we really wanted our bottle to look and feel 'organic', almost as if it were hewn from solid rock. This process took ages but, looking back, was well worth the effort.

Matthew had completed his initial designs for the logo, boxes and packaging which complemented the bottles and I began to truly believe we were on our way. Then another miracle - Roja confirmed that he would like to stock "Blessings" in his Urban Retreat perfumery in Harrods! My childhood dream was becoming a reality.

· · · · ·

"
The stunning blessings purple
in its original packaging

3

*I*N MARKETING the "Blessings" range I was all too aware that some producers care more about the mass market and do not necessarily remember the underlying reason for the existence of the brand. I determined to go against this and really make sure that "Blessings" fulfilled all my expectations and delivered my passion and memories in a package that everyone could enjoy.

I did not want to compromise on the quality of the high-end fragrance and so, when Roja and I started working on creating a beautiful yet affordable Blessings Eau de Parfum, we made sure that it still included rose de mai and jasmine de Grasse of the highest quality and, more importantly, that it delivered the fragrance of my life's journey so far; a fragrance that has sustained me for so long.

· · · · ·

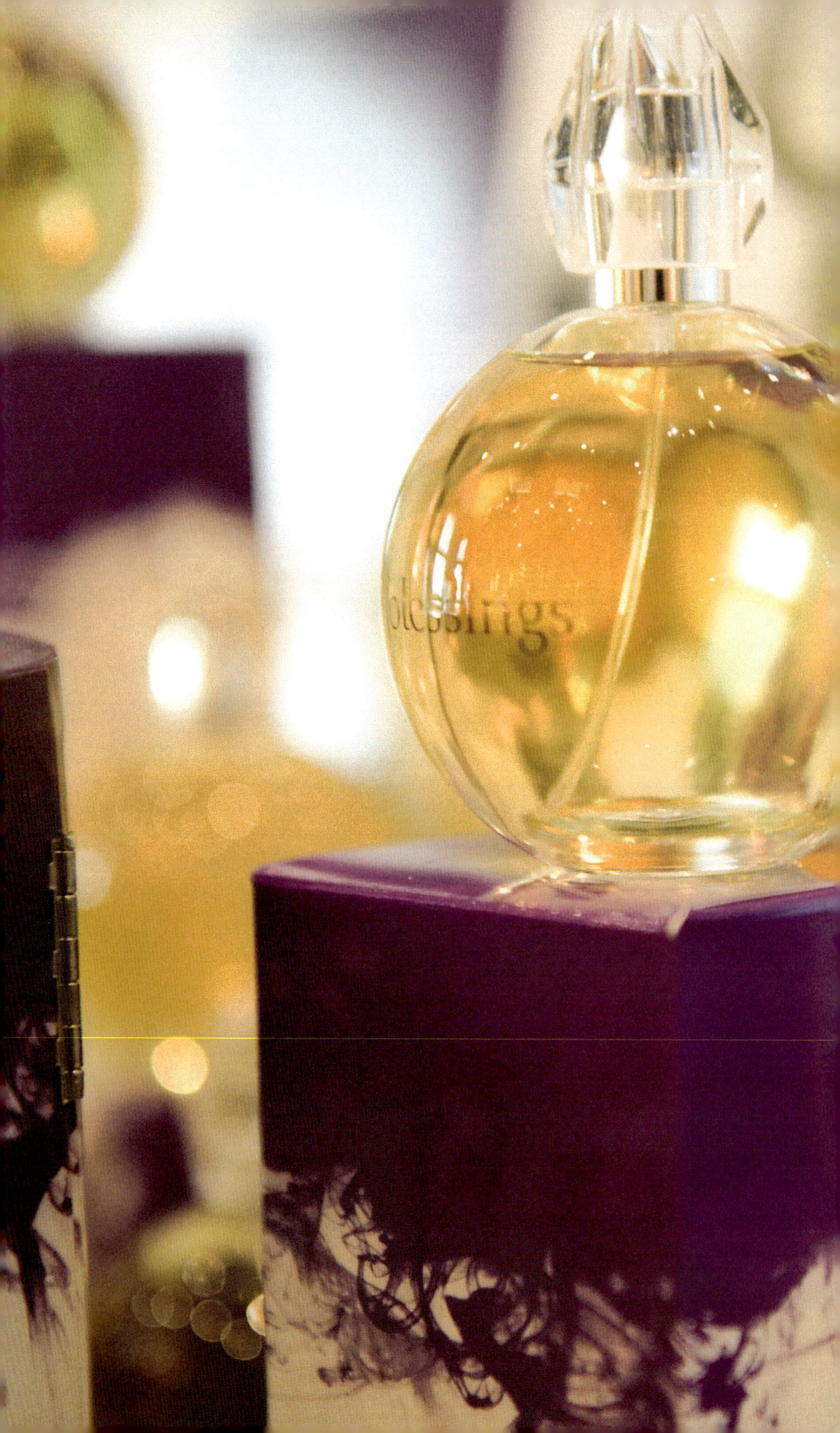
blessings

Eau de Parfum

4

WE DECIDED to launch "Blessings" to a select group of friends and to those who had been involved in the project from the start, at Browns Hotel in London in September 2010, followed by a trade and press launch at the Langham. This would coincide with Harrods stocking 50 bottles as a trial run. I was petrified but elated at the same time. Who would have guessed that I could have taken this dream so far?

Amazingly, nearly half the bottles sold on the very first day of launch and the remainder soon afterwards. I cannot adequately describe the pride I felt when I walked into the perfumery department at Harrods and saw my bottles on the shelf.

I remember standing beside my creation and seeing two gentlemen looking at and reading the silver writing "Blessings By Belinda Brown". It really hit me how far I had come.

Another thing that left me absolutely amazed was when I got a phone call from Harrods, informing me that they were sold out and needed to place in more orders as soon as possible for the clients on their waiting list! It was one of those moments when I wondered if the whole thing was a dream.

· · · ·

FORTY FIVE

5

SOON AFTER THE LAUNCH and, no doubt due to the publicity we generated, I was interviewed by a journalist working for the Nigerian airline, Arik Air.

My story obviously interested them as they were keen to promote Nigeria and Nigerians to a wider audience and soon after the article was published, they called me and "Blessings" was included in the duty free listings of the airline.

My vision when I worked at the airport all those years ago had finally come true.

blessings

FORTY SIX

blessings
BELINDA BROWN

Perfume and incense
make the heart glad,
but the sweetness of a friend
is a fragrant forest

blessings
BELINDA BROWN

A faithful person
will abound with blessings

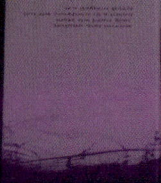

blessings
BELINDA BROWN
blessings
BELINDA BROWN
blessings
BELINDA BROWN
EAU DE PARFUM
Perfume and incense make the heart glad
but the sweetness of a friend
is a fragrant forest
blessings

Revelations
my inspirational journey

BLESSINGS is now winning worldwide attention with interested buyers from Switzerland, Russia, the Middle East and India. We launched it in Lagos in 2011 and it is available online at: www.blessings-perfume.com

I have also added 'Blessings Red' to the range. This equally exquisite parfum includes Rose de Mai and Jasmine and other notes as before but also includes Ylang Ylang (the essential oil distilled from the flower of the Ylang Ylang tree that is native to Mauritius) spices and clove. I also determined to produce a truly unisex product. Called "Pour Elle et Lui" it combines all the excellence associated with the blessings range in a fragrance that everyone will feel comfortable wearing.

Choosing a favourite perfume is a very personal thing and that choice almost always differs from person to person. One reason I am so pleased with the reaction to Blessings is because everyone seems so delighted when they try it for the first time.

• • • • •

As I said at the beginning of this book, the choice of name for my brand of perfume was easy.

Like most people, I have had my share of misfortune and heartache but surely I have also been blessed. Blessed with my parents (I am happy to say that my Mother is still alive and living in Yenagoa in the Bayelsa state in the Niger Delta) my family and friends and particularly for me, with my faith which has kept me going in times of distress and upon which I depend for guidance and inspiration.

If like me you believe in a divine presence looking after you and planning each stage of your journey, then my story is simply explained in that way. If you do not share my faith or indeed a belief in anything spiritual, then you must concede that I have been the beneficiary of the most amazing set of miraculous coincidences.

Whatever the truth, I would like to hope that we all could make the most of the lives we have been given, to seek a path to follow and to strive to succeed despite the odds stacked against us. Because, when we do finally succeed, we know we have truly been given a blessing.

. . . . .

FIFTY

blessings

"Perfume and incense make the heart glad, but the sweetness of a friend is a fragrant forest

"A **faithful** person will **abound** with **blessings**

*P*AUL COOPER ran a highly successful creative agency in London for many years and now acts as a freelance copywriter, editor and marketing consultant to a number of high profile clients in London and the South of England.

Paul met Belinda through his professional association with Matthew Marriott who designed the packaging and support material for the Blessings range of perfumes and also this publication.

Matthew and Paul have worked together for over 15 years on a wide range of creative projects.

www.thecreativestare.com
forest.marketing@btinternet.com
m.marriott@btconnect.com

Picture of the African sunrise page three
www.james warwick.co.uk

• • • • •

blessings
BELINDA BROWN